What To Expect Within

- o (Interview Sara for therapist's side)

Chapter 6 - Resources
- o Common sense test – Do you have it?
- o Problem solving test – Can you solve it?
- o Social etiquette
- o Downtime is important
  - ▪ Why
  - ▪ How

SOS Social Online Safety – For Tweens, Learning How to Protect Themselves from Both the Online/Offline Dangers.

www.kgwebsitedesigns.com

KG Website Designs

A company of KV@ Virtually Everywhere
1314 Calle Avellano
Thousand Oaks, CA 91360

kgarcia@kgwebsitedesigns.com

Cover by Katrina Garcia

You may be reading this and thinking, Social Safety, really? I know everything there is to know about social media. Heck, I even set up both my mom and dad's Facebook profiles. Which I don't even use anymore.

Besides, I know how to protect myself. You set up your profile, don't talk to strangers, block people you don't want anything to do with. Really, what can you possibly teach me that I don't already know?

Fair questions, but do you know what happens to your information online?

Do you know how a simple post can ruin your chances to get into the university or college you applied for?

Are you aware of the fact that a simple post may get you into trouble with the law?

There may be things in this book that doesn't surprise you, but it's worth the read if you plan to go to college or a university in the future. Plan to drive a car. Plan to have a job or god forbid, a career. Then you may take the time to invest in the read. It's not a long book, so what do you have to lose? A couple hours of your day? You may learn something new.

But if you believe you know everything there is to know about the internet and how it handles your information, then by all means don't continue to read. If you believe you know how to protect your personal information, if you even know what that entails, by all means don't continue to read. If you know everything there is to know about social media and profiles, then don't continue the read.

But if you want to protect what's yours from online hackers, read on. If you want to keep your reputation intact, read on. If you want to have a better chance of getting accepted to that university or college, read on. If you want to take back your power online, read on. If you're having issues with cyberbullying, read on.

Now that you've decided to read on, let's move forward.

So, let me give you a little background about me, the author. My name is Katrina Garcia, and I run a digital marketing firm where I help entrepreneur's and businesses create their social media channels, websites, and blogs. We also help them maintain these pieces by writing the content and providing the images and research to make their online business presence thrive. Now this may not mean that much to you, but the fact is, I've seen many of my client's and witnessed online activity that have broken up families, caused people to lose their jobs, had people arrested, and their information compromised by online hackers and thieves.

This may not sound like it means much to you now, but it will when we get into the juicy parts of this book.

I wrote this book to protect you, the reader. You may be 15, 18, 20 or mid 20's and your reading this book, and that was my plan. To have your age bracket walk away with some more knowledge that you can go back and teach your parents, sister, brother, grandma, grandpa, or maybe even your teacher. Either way, my goal is to have you realize that even though the internet is a great tool to play games on, Snapchat or Skype with friends it's also a really big place where your information can be compromised, taken or used against you.

What do I mean when I say, "Your Information"? Simply put, this information is what makes you unique from the next person:

- **Your social security number**
- **Your birthdate**
- **Your home address**
- **Your cell phone number**
- **Your credit card (if you're lucky enough to have one at this age)**

When I refer to this term, you will know what I mean. Some of you may not even have access to some of this stuff, because your parents have this under lock and key. But those who do, this information will follow you where-ever you go. When you get a job, when you get a driver's license, when you get a passport, when you apply to go to college, when you travel…..this information will be needed at one time or another. But also, this information can be used against you.

For example: Let's say that you're online conversing with a new snapchat friend and they ask you, "Hey I live in Bloomingdale Washington, where do you live?" What do you say? Do you give them the information? Now this may not be a really big deal upfront, but now they ask you, "So what's your address? Maybe I'll write you." Now at this point bells and whistles should be going off in your head. Why? Because everything you do is online. You send texts through your phone; you go online to converse with friends and family. So why does someone need your physical address to write you a letter. No one does that these days, right? And that's exactly what you should be asking yourself.

Lesson one – pay attention to the subtle, yet sometimes obvious signs.

Let me ask you, now that you know this, would you still give them your physical address? I certainly hope your answer is NO, because that's what mine would be. Why would someone want my physical address if we are talking online? Some obvious reasons that come to my mind, because I'm just a cautious person, is maybe they want my address to come by my house when no one is home and take all the good stuff, including, dare I say it, MY COMPUTER! Or maybe they want it to start stalking my every move. Or maybe they are trying to get more information to get to my parents who have all the money? You get the idea, right?

Now this information may not seem like much to you right now, but this information will be yours forever and will follow you everywhere you go. Now imagine if this information was stolen and now you go to open up your very first credit card only to find that you owe over $80,000 in credit card debt. Wait a minute!! I never opened up a credit card. How can I possibly owe that?

Every day the online flood gates are opened by hackers both big and small time players. But once the genie is out of the bottle, so is your information. Especially the more you use online sources. Even if you do everything right, doesn't guarantee your information isn't compromised by simply going shopping online or at the mall. Either way your information should be a sacred thing. It follows you for life, so protect it.

I recommend you talk with your parents about this more, because it's an important topic and you should be, yes dare I say it, caring for your information like your life depends on it, because it does.

Your information is used for a wealth of things, that you will find out as you grow up and experience life. But if you don't protect it now, that life may be compromised in more ways that you could possibly know now.

Here are just a few things in the future where your information will be used:

- Hospital stays
- Emergency room visits
- Doctor visits
- Credit card applications
- College applications
- Job applications
- Driver's license
- Buying a house
- Getting an apartment
- Buying a car
- Renting a car
- Renting a room
- Getting a passport
- Traveling
- Taxes
- Insurance forms

These are just to name a few, either way you get the picture.

Now let's get started into some further dangers you should be aware of. Yes, more. But that's the whole point of this book, to educate you. Once you have all the facts laid out before you, it will be that much easier to make better choices. Yes, I said it, better choices. But I promise you that this book will open your eyes and you will be that much better off than your peers.

Chapter 1
Dangers

Chapter 1 - Dangers

When you hear this word, what comes to your mind? Do you imagine a beastly monster hiding within your closet? Does it bring to mind similar images you may encounter during a game of Thrones? Either way, this is a word that can take on many forms.

- **Stranger danger**
- **Driving too fast and crashing**
- **Being hurt by another person either physically or mentally**
- **Being robbed**
- **Drowning in the sea or a pool**
- **Losing everything you have**
- **Being attacked**

No matter what this word conjures up for you, it's real. And when our bodies experience danger, we tend to go into a fight or flight mode. Simply put, this is when you hear the voice in your head screaming run, run…..and soon after your body follows. Or it could mean you freeze up and simply can't move or you go into fight mode and fight back. Either way, what causes you to experience danger in the first place is FEAR. Fear is a strong feeling that can be real or something we put there based on false information.

As your mind works through the fear it tries to decide whether the danger is real or not, at which point your body then reacts accordingly.

Haven't you found that you may be home doing your homework or listening to your tunes when you hear something go bang in the house? Your mind starts to wander. Do you go check it out? Do you stay put? Maybe it's the wind but wait it's not windy outside. No, it's the cat. But then you see the cat is in your room. Okay, okay it's your brother or sister playing a prank, but then you remember they stayed the night at their friend's house and aren't even home. Fear, that's what this is. You are working it through in your mind whether you should run or check it out. Usually, you go down the hall or down the stairs, turn on all the lights and find that something fell, or you can't even find anything. Either way, you appease your fear, go back to your room, but you keep listening just in case. You don't hear anything else. You close your door, lock it, put your headsets on and turn up the volume. Fear, gone.

My point here is that our minds can play tricks on us and usually makes more out of the situation than what really exists. This is fear – Fear of the unknown, fear of your mind trying to ration what you heard or saw. Either way, it's fear. But many times, there are dangers out there that are real and that's what I want you to pay attention to, especially those online. Because many of these dangers are hidden in places you least expect them.

Is my intent to scare you? Well, a little. Because if you don't take it seriously, it can become a real danger.

Laptop camera spying

Most of you have one, a laptop. And most of these are equipped with a built-in camera and microphone. But I bet you never really thought how someone can literally get access to your computer and spy on you through your laptop camera.

Scary I know, but factual. In fact, there is such a thing as "Sextortion" where a hacker gets access to your laptop webcam and video tapes you. Shortly thereafter you receive a notification to pay the designated amount or they will release the video across all social media.

Many times, you leave your laptop open and on so that you don't have to go through the process of signing on. Or many of you, admit it, don't even have a password set up to sign on. You simply turn it on and get started. Why waste precious time waiting for your laptop to boot up, right? Wrong!! This simple act opens you up to hackers because a computer that's on all the time gives them more time to find ways to access your computer.

TIP: *Put a fun sticker on the camera or a piece of tape. This will misconstrue the picture not allowing anyone to spy via your camera. Close your laptop so nothing can be seen, or simply shut it down every night. The last one is the one I highly recommend for a couple of reasons: Helps to reboot your computer for it to run much faster, and fewer chances of a hacker getting through. A powered down computer can't be accessed.*

Driving and texting

Now you've heard about this danger over and over. But it's worth repeating.

Some of you may not even have a license yet, but either way, these is now a huge issue that needs to be addressed.

Do you know that there are more lives lost and accidents, due to texting and driving, than driving under the influence of alcohol or drugs? This is a huge epidemic that, to this day, I still don't get why not only teens but parents do every day. In fact, while sitting at a red light I counted a total of 20 cars where I saw either someone texting while driving or talking on their phone, and it wasn't hands-free. Holding your phone and using your speaker is NOT HANDS-FREE.

When you drive a car, you are essentially driving a 3-ton object that outweighs 5 sumo wrestlers. You should be paying attention, not fiddling with your phone. Trust me, it only takes literally a second to take your eyes off the road to cause an accident.

Let's say you're driving along and your phone dings. It's your friend texting you. Well, you can answer back really quick. You pick up the phone and start texting, but then you look up and see a kid in a crosswalk. You slam on your brakes, but it's too late. You hit them. Now you have to suffer the consequences of your inactions. Court, losing your license, or even worse, going to the big house (jail) knowing that you either maimed or killed another human being. Now was that text really worth it?

You may be saying to yourself, "I know my mom and dad are always on my back about this?" or "But mom and dad do it." But that doesn't make it right.

Why else do you have to go through both a written and manual test before they let you have a driver's license? Because they want to know if you know how to drive. That you will be safe behind the wheel of a car. That you won't be a hindrance on the road. It's not just a matter of I passed or failed. It's a responsibility to every other motorist on the road. Does this mean everyone drives safely? Probably not, but at least it won't be you causing the accident if you pay attention and put the phone down.

TIP: *If you really have to return a call, then pull over to the side of the road or drive into a shopping mall and park. Now you will have all the time in the world to talk while staying safe for everyone, including you. Put your phone on car mode so that when friends or family text or call you it will send them a message stating that you are driving and will return their call when you've reached your destination.*

Now I realize that your parents may do the same thing, but ask you not to, so make each other a promise. If you catch your parents texting and driving or using their phone, that's not in a hand's free way, call them out on it. If your parents are reading this, sorry parents, but it starts with you. You can't expect your kids to do it if you aren't following your own rules.

Trust me, when I need to make a call or text, I don't do it while driving. I follow my own rules. I certainly can't expect you to read this if I don't. But ask any of my family and friends and they'll tell you the same thing. Be safe, don't text and drive.

Walking and Texting

Now we just went through the fact of texting and driving, but I bet no one ever told you to do the same when walking. Believe it or not, this can be just a dangerous. Why? Gee where do I start. Because there are even more obstacles to get through then driving. You have baby strollers, people walking towards you, behind you, bumps in the sidewalk, no sidewalk, crosswalks, cars when crossing the crosswalks, thieves looking for a chance to steal your purse or wallet......the list goes on and on.

TIP: *When you find you want to return a text, instead of stopping in your tracks to return it, go into a shop and sit down to type. Or simply find a wall to put your back up against to return the text. This way you stay safe as well as the people around you.*

Remember that you are not the only one on the sidewalk or in the crosswalk. You need to be aware of your surroundings, which can't be done if your texting and walking. Besides, how would you feel if you're walking along when the person right in front of you stops causing you to either run into them or having to walk around.

Rude Behavior

We've meet someone in our lives at one time or another who are just downright rude. But exactly what does being rude mean to you?

According to Wikipedia, the definition of rude is acting inconsiderate, insensitive, deliberately offensive, impolite, a faux pas, obscenity, profanity and violating taboos such as deviancy. In some cases, an act of rudeness can go so far as to be a crime, for example, the crime of hate speech. In simple terms, treat others how you would want to be treated. If you want to be treated with respect, then it has to start with you treating others with respect. If you want others to be kind to you, then you are kind. If you want others to be compassionate and listen, then you do the same. You get the picture. But with all the new smartphones out there many people; don't get mad but the stats prove it especially today's younger generation, are losing their ability to have face to face social connections. Why is this important? Because no matter how hard you try, everywhere you go you will have some face to face connection with people. The grocery store, the mall, the movie theater, school......each of these places are made up of a large group of people. With these people comes the responsibility to have good manners. That means you treat them with respect. What does that look like?

- When you talk with someone you look them in the eyes. Otherwise, you come off as shifty or mistrustful.
- You greet people with a smile and a kind hello. That doesn't always mean they won't respond in kind, but the more you do the more you will find people doing the same to you.
- Don't just stop when you have a crowd of people walking behind you. What if an elderly person or small child is behind you and falls because you simply had to stop to take a call or look at a picture your friend sent. If they are injured, it could be your fault.
- If someone says hi and smiles at you, do the same. Smile back and say hi. It won't kill you, and you may meet someone new that could be a huge influence in your life later down the line.
- If you don't have anything nice to say to someone, don't say anything. How would you feel if someone was downright mean to you and said hurtful things? You wouldn't like it, so do you think they will?
- When someone opens a door for you, say thank you. They don't have to go out of their way to be kind, but they are. Acknowledge that you appreciate their kindness. Or pay it forward and open the door for someone else.

These are simply common-sense actions, but you would be surprised how many don't even know this. I mean get real; life isn't full of Kardashions. Life is filled with real, honest, hardworking people that just want to be treated with kindness.

You may be asking yourself why I put this in the section of Dangers. Well, many of us have started losing our humanity. Literally the ability to be human to our fellow human beings. Simply put, our electronics are starting to turn us into egotistical jerks who only care about one thing, the next quick electronic fix. When you go through life with this type of an attitude life gives it back, and treats you like a jerk. If you find people are being downright jerks to you, maybe you should be looking at your own behavior.

Like I said before, everyone just wants to be treated equally and with kindness and you're no different.

So yes, this is a danger, as we continue down the spiral of electronics. Because someday, the electricity may go out and then your electronics won't work, and then you'll be left to fend for yourself, dealing with people face to face instead of text to text.....torture. Get over yourself and become a part of society and be kind, don't be another jerk. We have enough of them in the world, we certainly don't need anymore.

Be a part of the solution, not the problem, because anyone can be a problem. It takes someone special and kind to be the solution. Which segways into the next section.

Social Engagement

In today's world, we are filled with people who text, tweet, and post. But during this whole process, as I stated before, we tend to lose our social engagement with each other. Just like the monkeys, humans can't live on their own happily. They need interaction with others, they need that human touch or connection. Whether you believe it or not, you need the interaction of your friends. Why else does it mean so much to us to be wanted or liked by our peers or friends? Because we want to be accepted. But you can't be accepted if you hide behind your phone.

The fact that people have become more irritable or mean is because of how we tweet, post or text. We say things that we would never think about saying to some one's face. Why? Because if we saw their reaction, we wouldn't do it. Imagine before you hit the send button, how would you feel if you got the same message you were sending off? Would it hurt your feelings? Would it make you mad? Would it make you feel alone and disconnected? If so, then maybe you shouldn't send it....uh? Come on. This isn't rocket science it's called being human. Having feelings and knowing when to stop being a text, post, and tweet bully. And if that's your gig. Great. Just don't expect anyone else to like you or be kind because that starts with you. Before you can have kindness or be liked by others, you need to start being kind and like others. It's time to wake up and realize that the send button is all too easy to do. Be the person people look up to. Be the person everyone respects. Be the person everyone admires. Be you, a kind and accepting human being. Remember, what goes around, comes around. Usually in spades.

Start working on your social engagement and become engaged with other people face to face not text to text. Take the time to get to know people face to face, which is what we call the human factor. Which simply means being nice to your fellow man, woman, girl, boy or animal. If you can master this, you can master the world of being happy.

Area Attention

This is the last section in the danger chapter, but one of the most important as well. Even though we've discussed thus far the other dangers out there when using your phones, another one you want to be aware of is your area. Many people have gotten lost or walked into some dicey situations, simply because they didn't pay attention to their area. In other words, you need to be aware of your environment.

Pay attention to:

- The street names.
- Landmarks – Is there a coffee shop on the corner? Or maybe a gas station. What type of businesses or stores are in the area?
- How many steps or blocks does it take to get to your destination?
- If you are in a different city or state, pay attention to how everyone else is getting around. Are they using the subway? Are there a lot of public buses in the area?

Why are these important? Because when you pay attention to these known factors you will be better at recognizing when something doesn't seem right. When there might be a dangerous situation up ahead. However, if you are busy on your phone, you won't see this and may now find yourself in a dangerous area when it could have been avoided altogether if you had simply paid attention to your surroundings.

Let's look at another way. For those of you who play online games, what are the key things they teach you in these games? To pay attention to the thing behind the tree or the guy sneaking up behind you. These games are telling you to pay attention to your surrounds or your character dies or loses points. Imagine when you're out walking you do the same thing. You pay attention to your surrounding area.

Many kids, teens and even adults have been hit by cars or buses simply because they weren't paying attention when they were walking. I actually had a kid walk right into my car from a crosswalk, because he was so busy looking at his phone he never bothered to look up. Imagine if I hadn't seen him first? I even had a kid and his parent walk right in front of me in a parking lot, not once looking up. Don't make the assumption that a car, truck or bus sees you first. They have a lot to do when driving. They are working to maneuver the traffic, kids in crosswalks, traffic lights, looking in their rearview mirror and side mirrors. They don't always see you, so don't assume they do.

Just like there are accidents with texting and driving there are accidents with walking and texting, especially if you aren't paying attention to your area.

TIP: *Keep your phone in your pocket until you get to a safe zone, and only then, do you text or call. A safe zone is a shop or store you can go into to make a quick text or call. Of find a wall to lean against. This way you are safe to text and call away.*

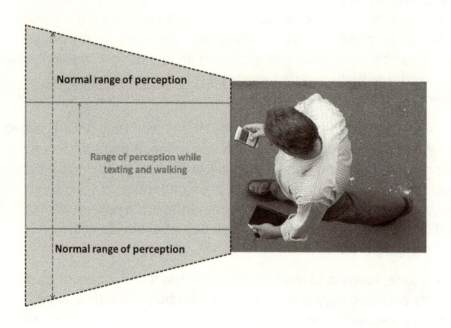

Chapter 2
Posting

Chapter 2 – Posting

We went through many of the dangers including some social dangers if we don't take the time to be human and have more face-to-face interactions. Now we will go over several issues when posting.

I realize that these days it seems anything goes. But what most of you don't understand now, is that your post will stay with you the rest of your life. Which essentially affects your future regarding jobs, college approvals, and in some cases financing. Keep in mind that this may not mean much to you now, but it should, because how you act or react online tells a lot about how you will deal with real issues as you get older. Which is what many future bosses, teachers, colleges, universities and friends will judge you by.

One key thing to remember is that "what you put online stays online FOREVER." It doesn't get deleted, just because you deleted it from your phone or computer. Once it's been put out into the social media atmosphere it's there to stay for anyone to see.

Now you may be thinking to yourself, "but if I block someone, I don't have to worry about them seeing my stuff." Wrong. Just because you blocked that person doesn't mean you blocked everyone within their social realm. In fact, most get caught doing illegal things online simply because they assumed only their friends could see what they posted. But what you don't understand is that everyone that one friend is connected to can see your posts, not just your friend.

TIP: *Before you hit the send button or post keep this in mind: if what you send can hurt or embarrass someone. DON'T POST IT. Or if what you post is read on the 9:00 pm news for your whole family, friends, classmates, teachers, and faculty to see and can damage your family, friends or your reputation, DON'T POST IT. Of if it can get you in trouble with the law, DON'T POST IT.*

Because regardless of what you believe, many of our Governmental departments including local police, FBI, and CIA are keeping tabs on everyone, on a regular basis, especially through social media because it's considered an open domain. This means it's open for anyone to see. Yes, you may have your profile set up so that only certain things are viewed by your friends and family, but that doesn't mean these agencies can't see it. In fact, they have programs in place that can pick up certain images, words, and posts based on the search. Trust me, your information is open for public consumption when you post to social media.

I'm not putting social media down; I'm simply making you aware of your actions online. Because that's what they are, your actions. If you get in trouble based on a post, you have no one to blame but yourself. Like I said at the very beginning of this book, educate yourself on the do's and don'ts of online posting so that you can do it without jeopardizing your future.

Let's go into a bit more depth of how to post the right way.

Spelling Effects

Today we have spell check on our phones and computers, but this is also causing many of us to lose the ability to spell. In fact, many online applications don't have spell check in place. Want to know why? Because they want to see if you truly know how to spell without having to rely on spell check.

Many jobs out there are looking for employee's who can do simple things, like spell and count. But the problem is that they aren't finding many who can without the spellcheck crutch.

Okay, so here's the mom speech – When I was in school, we didn't have computers. We had to know how to spell and count without the help of spellcheck or calculators. We had to learn to count back change when we worked in retail. We didn't have a cash register that told us what the change was. We had to figure this out on our own. When we filled out an application we had to know how to spell and had to write it out with a pen and paper. However, many of you have had the opportunity to learn on computers. But this has also brought up a whole new problem for businesses, because they are dealing with employee's who can't spell or count back simple change. May not be a big deal to you, but if you're the employee that can't spell or count, you'll be the one looking for another job, over and over and over until you do.

You may say, still not a big deal. But it will be when you need to pay for a car, insurance for the car, gas for that car, clothes, rent, food, you know the simple things in life that most of your parents or family are currently supplying for you now. But when you become of age, that soon changes.

When it comes to texting, this is a huge deal as we use acronyms or abbreviated words in order to get across a large sentence in 140 characters or less. Trust me, I get it. Say a lot with less. But in the real world, people don't say, LOL BFAW L8R. It works for texting, but not conversing.

TIP: *Pay attention to the words you misspelled and repeat back how to really spell it three times. This will help you in the future to spell it right the first time without having to depend on spellcheck and you will be a more sought-after employee or boss.*

Even though it may not seem important to you now, make it important. Because the spell hack will come back to haunt you later on in life. Trust me. I used to be the worst when it came to spelling. But I taught myself how to be a better speller, enabling me to be more employable, allowing me to have the funds to do what I want when I want.

Etiquette

Good spelling is one facet of posting, but another is proper etiquette. You may be asking yourself, what the heck is etiquette?

Etiquette is a code of behavior that delineates expectations for social behavior according to contemporary conventional norms within a society, social class, or group.

What does this have to do with posting or texting? Frankly, it has a lot to do with how you conduct yourself online.

Most of you who are reading this book are most likely already aware of this, as I'm sure your parents have taught you much of this when you go out to eat at a nice restaurant or attend the family Christmas party, go to the store, movies or simply going anywhere in public areas. I'm sure you've heard it.

"Don't smack your lips when eating."

"Stop whining."

"You need to use your inside voice."

"Don't embarrass me and behave."

"Don't run in the store."

"Don't touch that unless you plan on buying it with your own money."

Each time you hear this, your parents are trying to teach you how to act in public places. It may not seem like it, but it's true. They are simply trying to show you not to yell, not to touch things that don't belong to you and to behave properly while you're there. Simply put, etiquette. This is how we are taught to act in a restaurant, a movie theater, grandma's house, at the park, you name it, it applies.

As you are taught this when going to public places you should keep this in mind when posting, because there is such a thing as posting etiquette. In short:

- Don't post any personal information online.
- Don't make fun of people online.
- Don't have a full-blown argument with your friend online.
- Don't disagree about an issue online.
- Don't post inappropriate pictures online.

- Don't post you doing something illegal online.
- Don't be judgmental online.

These are simple things to abide by. Does this mean you don't have the freedom to express yourself? Absolutely not. This simply means that what you put online is in writing and can be used against you in the future. You may be saying, "what?"

What you don't realize it that we are in a society where everyone has an opinion these days but aren't really interested in hearing yours. They want you to hear theirs. As you can see this is very one-sided, and there are always two sides to a story and there are always two or more opinions. But this doesn't mean one is right and one is wrong, because everyone is an individual and deserves to say their piece. But when you do this online, now you are open to others who may disagree or be offended by your opinion. That is certainly their right, but there are some out there that will take your post and use it against you.

For example: When a couple is going through a divorce, they tend to lay out all their dirty laundry online. But what they don't realize is that the other person's lawyers can take that, because it's in writing, and use it against them in a court of law. Due to this, many divorces have ended very badly where some parents have lost custody of their kids due to their online posts. This may not mean much to you, but if you are the kid involved in the custody hearing, it will.

Here's another example: You go out tagging property with your friends and you post it online. Now you have cops knocking at your door to question you or arrest you due to your simple tagging. Why? Because it's illegal. Because you posted it online. Because now they have all the proof, they need to arrest you. BECAUSE YOU POSTED IT ONLINE.

Get the picture? Posting anything online is in writing, which can be used in any court of law because it's in writing. This doesn't mean all your posts are illegal, it simply means to be careful what you post.

 TIP: *If you have a beef with a friend either talk to them in person or on the phone. Don't do it online. If you*

disagree with someone's view, call them, don't do it online.

What to Post and Not Post

- Opinions matter but forcing yours on others is not freedom of speech.
- Don't assume people know what you mean. Remember they can't see your face and not always know when you are joking or not.
- What you post can affect your future such as inappropriate pictures (which we will cover later in the book, just keep reading.)
- Don't have an open argument online with your friend or family, because how you react to situations online tells a lot about how you will react in real life situations. This may not mean a lot to you now, but it will if you plan to have a job or apply to various different colleges.
- Don't say mean things online as this could be misconstrued as bullying.

Just as I mentioned early on in this chapter, think before you post. Remember if it can be seen on the 9:00 pm news for everyone to see, including your family, friends, and classmates, and doesn't look good for you, embarrasses someone you know or accuses someone of something that you don't have all the facts for, then don't post it. Because once something is posted online it stays online forever. Trust me, I will continue to say this throughout as I really want you to get this into your head. Remember your actions today will affect your tomorrows.

TIP: *If you aren't sure if your post will or can affect someone in a negative or hurtful way, have someone who is not close to the issue or problem read it first. Ask them, that if it was meant for them, how would they feel* *reading it. If they say, it would hurt or that's not a very nice thing to say. DON'T POST IT.*

Opinions Matter but Forcing Yours on Others is Not Freedom of Speech

I realize that in the great United States we have many freedoms that other countries don't. We have the freedom to express our religious preferences, how we feel about the Government, our opinions on world issues, or controversial issues. We have the chance to express and share our thoughts. This is a wonderful freedom that many of us use. But when you try to force your opinion on others, it's no longer a matter of freedom of speech. It's a way of bullying someone into believing what you believe. With these freedoms, everyone has the right to have their own opinions, and state their own thoughts.

Many times, you may see your relatives get into heated discussions about the Government or religion or disagreements on controversial issues. At these times, you may see some folks get very passionate about their beliefs. Which is a great thing! This is what makes us all individuals. But when someone states that what you believe is wrong, it's no longer considered freedom of speech. Not if someone is working to force you into believing what they think is right.

Keep in mind, this should not be confused with rules that are set forth for all of us to abide by. They are quite simple:

- Don't lay harm or try and kill someone.
- Follow the rules of the road when driving.
- Don't commit a crime.

These are only the basic ones, but this should be a conversation with your parents. Either way, remember that everyone has a right to their opinion. That opinion may not be what you believe in or what's right for you, but that doesn't give you the right to tell that person that their belief is wrong simply because you don't believe in it. That's called freedom. The freedom to think and believe what you feel is right for you. And the key words here are RIGHT FOR YOU. Remember not everyone is you. That's what makes us all individuals. That's what makes our country so great. It's filled with varying opinions, religions, and beliefs yet we all still manage to get along, for the most part. But the whole point here is to not force your opinions or beliefs on someone else.

You want to keep this in mind when you post. Not everyone will agree with what you have to say, doesn't mean that's a bad thing. It simply means we have a world of individuals with individual thoughts and beliefs. Doesn't make it right or wrong. Keep this in mind before you start down a path of accusing someone of having the wrong views.

Don't Assume They Know What You Mean

One key thing you want to remember when posting is never assume the person on the other end of that post gets your humor, or fully knows what you mean.

When we converse, we use our hands, body language, or certain expressions. One thing you have to remember is that only 20% of communication is verbal the other 80% is body language and facial expressions. Many times, someone may say something to you, but their body language or the tone of their voice says a totally different story.

Let me explain: Have you ever spoken with someone who says they aren't mad, but you can clearly see by the way they stand or the tone in their voice that they are? Of maybe someone tells you, "No I'm not hurt by what you said," but you can tell by the tears coming down their face or the way they are holding their arms they are very hurt. When you post something, the other person on that post cannot see your face or your body language and can only take the text you sent across at face value. A post is many times made up of words or letters. There are no emotions or body language to see. With this said, you can't assume that the other person on the other side of that post knows exactly how you feel unless you state it clearly with your words. But many times, this doesn't happen.

People have sent across a mean response that can cause a world of misunderstanding or hurt, but then they state, "I was just kidding." But the person on the other end of that post doesn't know this. You can't simply assume that the person reading your post knows how you feel.

You also need to realize that, if you can't put in words what you want to say, then maybe it's best you pick up the phone and talk to this person voice to voice, instead of sending a post or text.

Do you know that many arguments and hurt are caused by some simple misunderstandings or miscommunications? If you take the time to speak with this person either face-to-face or voice-to-voice you could avoid over 90% of issues, hurt feelings, and miscommunications. Unless you enjoy going through life with major drama every day. Personally, I want a life filled with happy times and as little drama as possible.

I'm sure you know friends who tell you that all the time, "Man I hate drama." Yet they are the ones who cause 90% of their own drama.

Let's face it, you have choices. You can choose to treat others how you want to be treated and get the same in return, or you can choose to be mean and get the same in return. No matter what you choose, the results are based on the choices you make. This is the same when you post online. If you decide to choose to say something deregulatory or mean, then don't be surprised when that someone gets upset or says something mean in kind. What you put out there is what you get back. Keep this in mind before you send any post, because the same is true here.

How What You Post Can Affect Your Future

Now we've spoken about what not to post and posting etiquette, but we really haven't discussed how some of the things you post can affect your future.

You may think that some of your posts are innocent enough, but what if someone gets fired over your post? What if someone gets hurt by your post and does something drastic, like tries to hurt themselves?

Believe it or not, if it's tracked back to you, you could be liable. What does that mean? Let's go into more detail.

First Story of Regret – Some time back a mother was upset at what one of her daughter's friends said about her, so she went online and pretended to be a 14-year-old boy. She got the girl interested in her and then started spreading untruthful and hurtful rumors about the girl. This girl successfully killed herself due to these posts. Soon after, the mother was brought up on charges for several violations: falsifying her identity, bullying a minor online, and manslaughter due to this girl's suicide. All because she was mad at what she said to her daughter. And she was an adult or supposed to be acting like one.

Second Story of Regret – A teacher posted online how much she hated one of her students in class, which she thought was posted to just her fellow colleagues in private, but found later that was not the case when this student's parent found out thanks to a friend online. Due to this, the teacher was fired from a job she'd had for over 30 years.

Third Story of Regret – Several girls managed to get a classmate to come over to one of their houses and proceed to beat her up – 4 against one. While this was happening one of them thought it would be funny to post it online. The very next week all of those who were involved, with the exception of the girl who was beat, were arrested and tried for battery and assault. Now they all have a criminal record that will follow them until the day they die.

Fourth Story of Regret – A college bound, good student, liked to party a bit too much. She posted pictures of all the various drinking parties she went to only to find that later when she tried to apply for various different colleges, not one of them accepted her. Why? Because of her online activity.

Many times, you may think that your post is innocent enough, but if it causes harm or hurts someone, it's no longer an innocent post. It's now considered cyberbullying (which we will go into more detail further in the book, keep reading there's more good stuff.)

I simply want you to understand that your actions online can affect your future.

How may you ask? Let's say you have stellar grades and have applied to all the best colleges, but a couple of years back you had a tiff with one of your friends online and said some really mean things. Now you find that every college you applied for denied your entrance. How could that be? Because colleges and universities keep tabs of your online activity. They want to see what type of a person you are, and your online activity tells a story. Tells them what type of a student you will be, what type of a person you are, and how you handle adversity. If your online presence doesn't look so good, then your chances of getting in won't look so good either. Regardless of your grades.

Now I know this may not mean that much for some of you at this point, but it will when that time comes, and that's getting a job. Believe it or not, they check your online presence as well, which could mean the difference of getting the great job to possibly having to settle for the not so great job. As with colleges and universities, they check your social media channels. They look at who you follow, who follows you, what type of images or pictures you post or the type of friends you hang out with. Do you keep your personal life, personal, and not out there for all to see? Do you handle situations with care and grace? Who do you hang with online? Who are your friends? Do they party a lot? Do they post content that is questionable?

Your online presence, social media channels, what you post, paints a picture of what type of person you are. How you handle yourself under stress. How you handle tricky situations. How you express yourself. All of these tell a story about you and who you are as a person. You may be thinking to yourself, "but my Facebook or Instagram or Snapchat has nothing to do with who I am." But in reality, it does. It shows others what you do for fun, what type of family environment you have, how you view the world, but more importantly how you conduct yourself online. Because this is what future job opportunities, future college and universities, and possibly how future friends judge you. Thus, the importance of your online presence and how you conduct yourself based on your posts and images. Check it out for yourself. Look at one of your friend's social media channels and what they post. What type of images do they post? Do they argue every point a friend makes? Do they agree with everyone? Do they block content or simply don't care who posts or what they post? Do they follow political agendas? Do they believe in the same things you do? Do they have the same likes as you? Do they say kind things to others or simply put everyone down? Because this is how people judge you as well.

In fact, before I get connected with anyone, I check out their feeds, their imagery, and views. If it is someone I want to follow, then I do. But I don't just accept every friend request or follow everyone on social media. I'm careful of who I follow and accept. Why? Because this reflects on me and how I'm viewed. Some of you may say, why should that matter to you? But if I have client's viewing my information or a possible future client, I have the possibility of losing that client simply by my posts and who I follow. Like I said before, this may not mean anything to you now, but trust me, it will when you're ready to get a job or apply to a college or university. It will matter when you are trying to get into a specific club and committee. It will if you decide to run for office or apply for a Government position. It will if you decide to become a teacher or principle of a school. It will if you decide to start your own business. Because what you post online is viewed by everyone, and that's how they will be judging you. Based on your online friends and posts. I recommend you are very careful on what you post online because you don't know how or when it may affect your future.

Legalities of Your Online Actions

Part of the things we post online not only can be judged by others, it can and will be seen by law enforcement or attorneys. You may not be aware of this, but many local law enforcements watch online activity. They look at anything that can either help them find a perpetrator or possible felon. What does this mean to you?

Let's say that you and your friends go out and video tape you doing things that aren't legal, (I would go into detail here, but I don't want to give you any excuse to do so) and one of your buddies posts it on his or her social channels. You may think. Not a big deal, right? Wrong. Because law enforcement has ways of picking these things out amongst thousands and thousands of online profiles. And now your buddies simple post has you all in trouble, because they have a video of all of those who were involved. All the proof they need to arrest you and your friends.

I must admit that this is one of those things I really don't get with the upcoming generation. You go out and do something wrong or illegal and then you post it online for everyone to see. But what astounds me even further is how surprised or shocked you are when you're caught. Really? You posted it online.....for everyone to see......what did you think would happen? It's similar to someone videotaping themselves doing something illegal and then sending it to all the local news channels to show on TV. Because that's what social media is. It's similar to TV, where a large audience can see what you did and when you did it. If you get caught....maybe you shouldn't have posted it?

Then there's the story where you are caught because someone, you don't even know, was videotaping it from their phone because they knew it would go viral. I mean look around you, just about everybody has a phone that can take pictures and video. Plus, the majority of the population out there has some type of social channel in place, Twitter, Facebook, Snapchat, Instagram, Pinterest.....the list goes on and on. Even if you are careful of your actions, you can still be caught off guard by someone else's actions.

Let me explain further; remember the Olympic swimmer Michael Phelps? He had a ton of endorsements from some really big-name companies. But because of a simple picture of him at a party getting caught smoking pot, that he wasn't even aware was taken or put online, he lost the majority of his endorsements. He had to come out with a televised apology, and he had his day in court. But the list goes on how one simple act changed his life forever.

I realize this tends to make us a bit paranoid, but in today's day and age with cell phones everywhere, is it a chance you want to take? Besides, if you aren't doing anything wrong, if you behave yourself in public areas or parties, then you really don't have anything to worry about. But it's up to you on who you hang out with and how you conduct yourself, no matter where you are, that will be judged or possibly posted. Here are a few things to keep in mind:

- Ask yourself before you get involved with anything, how will this look should it get posted online?
- Pick your friends wisely and the places you hang out.
- Really read your posts before you post them.
- Express yourself well in a way that tells your true story.
- Be creative but be smart about it.

What comes across on your social channels can't always be controlled by you. There will be times you have to block a friend or take a post down, but as long as you use common sense knowing that everyone can see every post, you should be able to make the best choices for you. Just remember, it's your online presence. What you do with it is up to you, but don't be surprised if something may come back to bite you in the butt.

Chapter 3
Pictures/
Videos

Chapter 3 ~ Pictures/Videos

We've talked about posts, we've talked about some of the dangers, but one of the key things that most people don't realize is pictures and videos. These tend to get more people in trouble than words, because as the saying goes, "a picture is worth 1,000 words." This really rings true when it comes to posting images.

With posts, they are simply words that many can take one way or another, but images or pictures are what they are. An image of an incident, party, crime, kindness, love, doing for others, helping someone….the list goes on and on. But the beauty of images is that one simple image can tell a whole story without having to use a single word. On the other side of that, it can also tell a story that may have or may not have really happened. Let me explain; let's say that you are at a friend's house with a bunch of your other friends. You have a glass of soda in your hand, but surrounding you are friends with beer bottles in their hands. Someone takes a picture of you all, but you always tend to close your eyes when pictures are taken. Now you know you didn't drink at the party, nor were you drunk. But the picture says another story, because all your friends are drinking, and you look kind of drunk based on your eyes being half closed. You swear up and down that you weren't drinking that you weren't drunk, but based on the picture, it tells another story. Even though you weren't partaking in the drinking, it's automatically assumed you did based on the evidence in the picture. Everyone else has a beer in the picture. But you say you had a soda. Sure, maybe you were the only one drinking the hard liquor. But I wasn't drinking. Then how come you look like your drunk? Because I closed my eyes when the picture was taken. Sure you did. See how things can be misconstrued simply based on the circumstances within the picture? Even though it was innocent enough on your part, others don't see it that way.

Then there are those pictures that have been modified or tweaked that tell a total lie. Either way, pictures are powerful as are videos. Ask those who have lost their jobs, got kicked out of school, lost a friend or a loved one all based on a picture that was posted. As I mentioned in earlier chapters, we live in a different world than the one I grew up in. Today, just about everyone has a phone that has a camera on it, and with this technology, we have the capability of taking a picture or video that can go viral online. With this in mind, we also need to be aware of our surroundings and who we call our friends or where we spend our time. Just because you may not be part of the group that may partake in a sticky or compromising situation, doesn't mean you are innocent. Many accuse you simply by association. Simply put, people tend to judge. Admit it, you do the same. You judge the new kid on the block. The new kid in school. The girl who hangs out with the wrong crowd. We all judge based on looks, actions, and the people you hang out with. I'm not saying to not live your life. I'm simply saying that you can't be upset when someone judges you based on the people you hang out with, as this tells others what type of person you are based on your friends and acquaintances. I'm not saying it makes it right, I'm simply stating facts. Let's face it, you've done the same thing at one time or another. I've done it myself. But we can't judge people by the cover, so to speak. We need to look at all the facts before we make a judgment call. But the majority of human nature is to judge first and then ask questions later. Same stands true with social media. People judge you based on your posts and your friends' posts, they judge you based on your pictures and videos posted. They judge you on your likes and dislikes. They judge you on who you follow, your favorite band, singer, e-books you like to read, games you like to play, you name it, they judge it. Why give them more reason to judge? If you post with good intentions, not based on judging or being mean yourself, you should be safe. But when it comes to social media, there are no guarantees.

Picture Says a Lot About You

As I stated, pictures tell a story without having to say a thing. That's why you need to be careful of the pictures you post. This includes your profile pictures.

Girls – Trying to look sexy by making gestures or showing your cleavage isn't cute. Why? Because this is what others see:

- Wow, she's probably easy to get in bed.
- I bet she gives out.
- I think I'll start a conversation to see how far she's willing to go.
- Let's see if I can get her to trust me so that I can get her to come with me away from her family.

You essentially open yourself up for online predators. You can read more about what to look for here: http://www.familysafecomputers.org/predators.htm

Boys - Same thing goes for you. The gang gestures don't help your chances when you want to move onto a better life.

These images tell a picture, and even though you think it's really cool it tends to get you in trouble or into situations that can be difficult to get out of. Ask those who have gone before you and they'll answer they wish they had never gone down that road.

Keep in mind people, we all have choices. We can choice to do the right thing or go along with the group mentality. Either way, your choices have consequences. You may not see it now, but trust me, you will face the music and it won't be pretty, nice, neat, cool, happy, fulfilling or fun. We all make mistakes, but what we do to rectify those mistakes says a lot about you as a person. Think about it before you post it. Just because your friends do it, doesn't make it right. And here's a powerful thought; if they were true friends, they wouldn't ask you to do something that doesn't feel right to you. If this is the case for you, maybe you should find some real friends before they bring you down.

When it comes to profile pictures, pick something that's appropriate for you and shows the real you, not the one who's trying to impress their friends. Because these images will follow you for the rest of your life. Why? Because what goes online stays online forever. Trust me I will keep saying this throughout until you really get this set in your head.

Here's a motto you should always live by:

Think before you talk.
Think before you act.

Because if you do, 9 times out of 10 you won't do it, because you know deep down inside it's wrong for you.

Keep in mind that your life is just that, yours, so be smart about it. You have long lives to lead and by making good choices you will lead much happier and fulfilling ones. Think before you post any image or video.

What Others See Including Your Parents/Friends/Police

Believe it or not many have lost really great paying jobs based on photos or videos they've posted online.

- Teachers have lost their job and can no longer teach.
- Parents may lose a legal case based on posts.
- People have gone to jail based on posts.
- Predators have ruined many lives.

Don't be another stat on a graph showing how another fell prey to a predator or another fell prey to peer pressure. Be yourself, which many of you may still be trying to figure out. But remember that you have choices, good or bad, you make the choice on what you do with your lives and this includes your online presence. Choice wisely.

Remember that the friends you follow or become your online friends can see everything you post, including everyone they are attached to. That's a long list. It could mean up to 500+ people may see your post, image or video and one of these people may happen to pass it onto your teacher or your parents or your local police. Just don't post anything that can get you in trouble, including posts. For Example: Let's say you are at the mall when you called in sick to school that day. You take tons of pics of you buying clothes, eating, and hanging out with your friends. Until your post gets back to your teacher or your parents. Now you get an unexcused absence and grounded by your parents. Was the mall trip really worth it? You may think you will never get caught, but they all eventually do. Maybe not today or tomorrow, but it will come one day and when it does it won't be fun or cool.

This is exactly why I decided to pull this book together in the first place. After speaking with several students over the years it made me realize that you all know the internet really well. You all know how to set up a social profile and get your pictures posted. But what really surprised me is how little many of you know regarding safety and how your posts, images, and videos are seen.

You may think I'm just throwing a bunch of crap at you, but everything in this book is true and has been proven over and over. Trust me, I'm writing this to make you think before you post anything. Make you realize that not just your close friends see it, everyone sees it, whether you believe this or not, it's a fact. Which can and will affect your future in one way or another.

- It could mean the difference of keeping a really good friend or losing one.
- It could mean the difference between being safe or getting in trouble that can't be simply ignored.
- It could mean the difference of getting that job you really wanted or not.
- It could mean the difference of the life you always dreamed of or your worst nightmare.

In today's world, everyone is not only judged by their outer shell, their accomplishments, but their online presence. Make it a good presence and you have a great chance for a strong future.

What also astounded me about today's youth is how easily you post yourselves doing illegal things. Like you almost want to be caught, pay restitution or put in juvie. But really gets me is how many of you are surprised someone found out. Um…you posted it online. Remember? For everyone to see. Remember? You thought it would be cool. Remember? And now you got caught. Who do you have to blame? YOU. You did the crime, now you get to do the time because you posted it online.

How You Will Be Judged Based on Your Picture

We kind of covered this in a previous section - Picture says a lot about you. We talked about your profile pictures and how this can paint a picture of you without even having to say a thing. You want it to reflect the best you, not a cool you, not what your friends think of you, you. I guess the question here is for you to figure out: who are you?

-   What do you like?
-   What do you dislike?
-   What type of people do you like to hang out with?
-   What do you do really well?
-   What types of talents do you have? Can you sing, make the biggest bubble gum bubble in the world, paint, draw, are great at math, a future Bill Gates or Steve Jobs?
-   What makes you tic?

Once you figure this out you can pull together a great profile for all to see. But you also must remember that your pictures need to reflect this as well. The real you.

Who You Follow Affects You

We aren't only judged by the pictures we post or the posts in general, we can also be judged by the people we follow. Think about this for a moment. What if you hang out with a crowd that drinks a lot, but you've never touched the stuff? Because you are seen with the group, people assume you do the same things they do. Whether you do or not, that's how you are viewed. Same thing goes with your social media. People judge you by the people you follow. Based on this, you also have to think twice as to the people you follow.

Let's get really deep into this subject. Let's say that you have a friend that seems to be more outspoken and tends to say things that aren't always met with the best comments. But because you follow them, people assume you have the same views, you feel the same way or have the same outlook on life. Once again, you may think this doesn't really mean much to me, but it will when it's time to get a job or apply for college. It will matter a lot.

TIP: *Look at those you follow, check out their posts and images. Do they represent the image you want to put across? Or do they contradict who you really are? If they do, maybe it's time to let them go and unfollow or unlike.*

Just remember, anytime you go out of the house and deal with people you are dealing with people who judge. We all do it. We judge based on your appearance, we judge based on who you are hanging out with, we judge based on how you talk or what you say. We are all human and tend to judge. Whether we like to admit it or not, we all do it. Why give them more to judge? Simply put, be yourself but also be true to yourself by the people you hang out with. Are they really true friends? Do they have your best interest in mind, or do they have their own agenda? Hang out with people who can enhance your life, not bring you down.

Safety

Now we've gone through some of the dangers of posting, images, how people tend to judge you based on who you follow or follow you, but the biggest key I want to push home is how you can protect yourself with various different apps, software options, and protecting your information. Out of all the chapters and topics we've covered thus far, I believe this is the most important. Why? Because the whole point of this book is not to simply make you aware, but to teach you how to protect yourself. I realize that you have control to a certain degree, but as I stated in previous chapters, knowledge is power. I repeat, knowledge is power. The more you know, the more prepared you will be to make the best choices for you.

Even though the internet has:

- A ton of information.
- The ability to share your thoughts.
- Help you get around town.
- Shop online for your favorite game, computer, shoes, clothes, etc.
- Get the answers you need to get your homework completed.
- Help solve disputes on who was the voice of Darth Vader.
- Find the perfect photo to send your friends.
- Upload and share your pics.

Pretty much whatever you want to know, buy or investigate it can be found online. We go to the internet for a variety of reasons. But whatever your reasons to visit the world-wide web do you know how to protect yourself along the way?

Even though this technology has been around since the 70's, it was most likely way before you were born, so you've been used to getting information quickly at the click of a button. But with this technology also comes the scams, hackers, and stalkers. Because regardless of your positive outlook on life and trust in mankind, there are people out there that only have one thing in mind.

"How can I make a quick buck?"

"What can I do to get notoriety for all to see?"

Because in most cases, this is the predominate reason scammers and hackers work to get access to your computer and your information. You want to protect yourself. But many times, when I talk with Tweens they usually state they know everything about computers. Yet they know very little about safety. Sure, they can get around on a computer quickly, get things set up quickly, get acclimated to the interface quickly, but the one thing they never pay attention to is how to protect their information.

When you open your computer for the very first time, in most cases, your new system comes with preloaded virus protection, but how protected are you really?

- Do you pay attention to the updates that you receive or just ignore them?
- Do you ensure you have both virus and malware installed or just assume what's installed is good enough?
- Do you assume just because you have an iPad or iMac your virus free?
- Do you assume that every site you go to is safe?
- Do you assume that every app you download is safe?
- Do you pay attention to the sites you go to?

If you can say yes to even two of these questions, then you are essentially opening yourself up for hackers and scammers alike. Keep in mind that there are reasons why companies work so hard to put forth updates. They are in place, because of an issue or possible security breach and they have found a fix to protect your system or computer.

Remember, when you go online to download an app or software program, or simply opening up an email you take a chance of infecting your computer. You give them a chance to capture all of the information you have noted on this computer including your name, address, phone number, your parent's credit card number or yours, and in some cases your social security number. If you frequent the internet you need to protect yourself and your info. There are simple ways to do this, which we will cover in depth in the next chapter.

Chapter 4
Safety

Chapter 4 - Safety

As I mentioned in earlier chapters, you really need to pay attention to who you share your personal information with. This means your address/phone numbers/age/birthdate/social security/driver's license (if you have one). All of this information should be kept in a secure place and never given out online. Especially if you are under the age of 18. You may hear this from your parents as well, but there is a reason for this. Trust me, it's not to be a pain or take away your freedom, it's to protect you. Why? Because currently, your age group (12 – 21) is the most targeted group when it comes to scams and credit card fraud.

Many times, you won't even know that your information has been hacked until you start to get credit cards, look for an apartment, or buy your own car for the first time. Due to the fact that before you can acquire any of these things, they do what they call a credit check. This is when they check to see if you have any outstanding balances or bills that were never paid. You won't find out how much damage someone has done until you start trying to build your own credit. It's been proven that your age group is targeted, based on this very fact. You simply won't know how much damage has been done until you start filling out your very first credit card application or apartment lease. Not a real good way to start your future, right? But you can do your best to help prevent it, by keeping your personal information, well….personal. Only you should have access to this. Including when you set up your social media, go online and order something, or when someone starts asking for this type of information. You may be thinking to yourself, so why do I care about this now? Because it can take years to clear up your credit and you will find out soon enough, how important your credit score is as you try to attain it. I recommend you speak with your parents or someone you trust who can help you better understand this. All I can say is to keep it protected.

Now you also may be asking yourself, "but in order for me to get a social channel set up, they ask me for my birthdate." Yes, this is also to ensure you are old enough to utilize the social channel. But there are ways to keep this information a secret without the whole social media world knowing about it. But we will cover this further in this book.

 TIP: *Keep your social security in a safe place, such as a locked box. Or with your parents. Don't divulge your personal information online.*

Apps That Can Help Protect Your Info

There are many Apps out there that can help you protect your information and files, but you need to download them first. I recommend the following:

- Virus Protection for both computer/phone ~ AVG
- Malware Protection for both computer/phone – Malwarebytes
- Password App to store all your passwords in one place – Roboforms

You can get the free version or pay roughly $35.00 for more robust protection. Either way, just be sure you download some type of virus, malware, and password vault protection on all your platforms: phones, computers, tablets, gaming machines etc. This will help to keep your files and information protected on each device. Granted there are a ton of different options out there, however, the above apps have not let me down thus far. Just make sure you pick one that will protect all your devices.

Email vs Texting

We covered this in a previous chapter as well, but here's some info you may want to consider before you send a text or email. Whatever is in writing can be used against you in more ways than one.

Keep in mind that anything in writing, whether that be a text or email can be used in a court of law. Why should this matter to you? If you have a dispute with a friend and do all of your arguing via text or email, that same friend can take you to court for cyber bullying. Yes, I said it. Cyberbullying. Since this is an issue that seems to be a rampant problem, both schools and parents aren't taking this issue so lightly anymore. The next time you have an issue with a friend, work it out face-to-face. And this doesn't mean that you do or say something stupid and video tape it, because this can be used as evidence in a court of law as well.

I recommend you try to work it out amicably. Not sure what this word means? Look it up. Either way, the goal is to solve your issues in a kind way without name calling or becoming physically hurtful. If you learn how to do this well, you will get through life much easier with any future disputes. It's not a matter of who wins or who loses. It's a matter of who can be the bigger person in this scenario. Yes, I know that your parents may have told you the same thing, but it's true. By learning how to solve issues with finesse and tact you make yourself a valuable commodity for any business, because this is what true leaders do.

TIP: *Before you start to argue In a text or email, pick up the phone and set up a time to talk face-to-face. It might seem like a scary thing to do, but this is what makes you capable of handling strife, complicated issues, and hone your negotiating skills.*

Written vs Verbal

This ties in with the previous section. As we pointed out, it's best to use verbal communication when working to resolve an issue or argument. However, there are times where a written option may be a better bet. For instance, if you want to prove someone is picking on you, tell them to send it in a text or email, otherwise, you don't want to hear it and walk away. Now you have the proof you need.

Blocking One Doesn't Block Them All

Just because you block someone on your social channels, such as Facebook or Instagram, doesn't mean you've blocked them out completely. Keep in mind that they have friends who may be connected with you and can still see your feeds or posts. Especially if they have chimed in with previous posts you've put out there.

Simply blocking one person doesn't mean you block their circle of friends. You can block their feeds and their profile, but this doesn't mean they can't see what you post. They can always get your posts via their connected friends.

Consider it this way; when you see a spider web you see many types of bugs within that spider web and how every strand is interconnected. Essentially this is the same configuration many social media channels use. Once you get connected with one person, you are essentially connected with all of their 500 other friends as well. Even though you may block one friend, you are still connected to the 499 remaining friends.

 TIP: *Be sure you know who you are connecting with before you do.*

What Goes Online Stays Online Forever

This is one you want to remember over and over. Keep this handy on your computer as a note on your phone, wherever you see it at all times. Because what goes online stays online FOREVER. That's right, forever. No matter if you delete it or not it stays in cyberspace forever. For example, you text someone and delete it from your phone, that text is still out there in cyberspace. Same thing with a post, text, or email. How can this be? Because whether you believe it or not, each time you access a social channel, your phone or computer, there is a server that is keeping track of everything you save or delete. That server is usually based with the company providing the service or access.

What does this mean to you? Let's say you got into an argument with a friend and sent a bunch of scathing text messages. But you deleted them off your phone and you're no longer friends. However, the parent sees one of your texts and starts questioning who this so-called friend is? Now they want to press charges, known as cyberbullying. They put forth a court order to get all of your text records from your service provider (Verizon, AT&T, Sprint, T-Mobile, Virgin Mobile…etc.). Now they have all the evidence they need to start a case against you. Why? Because it's in writing. Now do you get it?

Whether you delete it or not, it's still always accessible in one way or another.

TIP: *I mentioned this in a previous chapter, but it's worth mentioning again. If your text or post can be seen by the whole world on the 9-clock news and can either ruin or hurt someone based on the words within, DON'T POST IT OR TEXT IT OR TWEET IT OR EMAIL IT!*

What Goes Around Comes Around

Based on what I've covered in this chapter you must remember that what comes around goes around. What does this mean?

Let's say that you said something hurtful to someone in front of the whole class. It may not happen in the same day or several days later, but it will happen where you will be put in the same situation, but on the other side. Now instead of you saying the hurtful thing, someone is saying it to you in front of the whole PE class. Or someone you really like throws hurtful words your way. One way or another it comes back to bite you in the ass. The key is to keep these four things in mind before you even open your mouth or mind:

(Brought to you by the Four Agreements by Miguel Ruiz)

1. Be impeccable with your word.
   In other words, don't say mean things to anyone.
2. Don't take anything personally.
   Just because someone puts forth hurtful words, may not have to do with you at all. Don't take it personally.
3. Don't make any assumptions.
   A lot of times we ASSUME that they are talking about us or saying something mean. They may be talking about someone else altogether. Either way, don't let it get to you. Just walk away.
4. Always do your best.
   If you always do your best at everything you do, how can you go wrong? Sure, you may make mistakes here and there, but that's what mistakes are, lessons for you to learn how to do it better the next time.

I realize that there are times when it seems the whole world is against you. Like you don't have any friends or someone on your side. Just remember that these are all thoughts based on fear. Fear of not being wanted, fear of not being liked, fear of being alone....whatever that fear may be, that's usually what makes us lash out or hurt. FEAR.

Each time we are given a challenge this is a chance to learn. Learn how to do it better next time. But we need to be receptive of the lesson and not continually keep doing the same mistakes over and over. Learn your life lessons well, so that you don't have to repeat them.

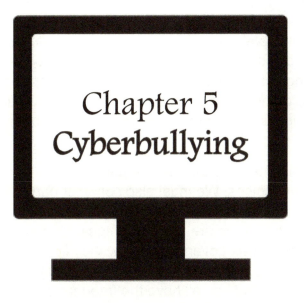

Chapter 5
Cyberbullying

Chapter 5 – Cyberbullying

This has been a hot topic across many schools and even businesses, where many cases have either ended in tragedy or for many who have persevered. But with this topic also comes responsibility. Responsibility for your actions, what you say, what you text, what you post. As I've discussed throughout this book, you need to realize that your personal power is just that, yours, and we must not work to force others to see things our way. Because the world is made up of unique individuals with their own mindset, ideas, strife, problems, rewards, we need to realize that it is not up to us to try and mold people. Our strengths and weaknesses are just that, ours, and they should never be blamed on others. That includes blaming mom and dad. Are they a big part of who we've become? Absolutely, and so are your peers, classmates, and friends. But ultimately, it's up to you on what you do with your lives, whether you decide to be the bully, the victim or yourself. Now I'm not condoning this option, be the bully, but I'm simply stating that it's up to you on how you conduct your life, who you hang out with, who you decide to become friends with, and what paths you decide to take shapes your life.

Each of us has one thing that no one can take away from us, our minds and our choices. We must also consider ourselves lucky enough to live in the U.S. where freedom of speech, many times is taken for granted. There are many countries out there where they have no say over their government, how they live or what type of job they hold. Yes, I'm on my soapbox again, but I want you to really understand that you all have the freedom of choice. Who to choose as a friend, what job you want, what school you want to attend, what car you want to eventually drive, what food to eat, where to live when you're old enough to do so, etc. The key is you have choices. How you make these choices are completely up to you. But you can't lay blame on others based on choices you've made. You may be asking yourself, so what's the big thing about choices? Because when we talk about cyberbullying you have the choice to be a victim or do something about it, and this doesn't mean doing harm to yourself. It means taking action. I mean turning off your phone, closing your social account, getting a new number, speaking with someone who can help. It means taking responsibility for your life and not allowing a cyberbully to take away your personal power. Now we will go into more depth in the coming sections, but I really want to reiterate, that your personal power is yours to either keep or allow it to be taken away. But these are choices you have, and yes, they are choices. No one can take your personal power if you don't allow it, and the key word here is YOU.

Everyone is just as important as the next, and everyone matters. As they say, these days, lives matter and this rings true as well when it comes to cyberbullying. Your life matters no matter what someone may say about you. Also, keep in mind that cyberbullies use words or photos to hurt. They want your power, see you as an easy target, and take aim at your character. Cyberbullies prey on those who give away their power to others. They prey on those who don't have a lot of confidence in themselves. They prey on those who don't fight back. They prey on those who they feel they can control. Don't be a cyberbully victim. We will go over several ways to regain your personal power and resources to help you do just that. Read on my tweens.

Who to Tell

Cyberbullying can take many forms.

- Texting nasty rumors that are untrue or distorting the facts.
- Sending photos that you weren't even aware were taken.
- Posting to your social channels.
- High jacking your social channels.
- Saying things at school.
- Starting rumors at school.

But as I stated before, cyberbullies prey on those they can control. That's how they get their power. But what you don't realize is that cyberbullies are bullies, because of their own lack of worth. You see, they want your power because they have none of their own.

Bullies wouldn't be bullies if they had true confidence in themselves, because there would be no need to do so.

Don't you have school mates or friends that are confident in themselves and never seem to allow others to get to them? Those who can be called a name, but just brush it off and walk the other way? Those who don't seem to care if someone makes fun of them? These are individuals who have personal power and don't allow others to take it. They know who they are, and more importantly, they are truly happy with who they are becoming. Do they have moments of doubt? Of course, they do. Do they have moments of weakness? Of course, they do. But they don't allow these to define them as a person. They get past them, they work through them, they become a better person because of them. We all have these opportunities as well, but we've allowed others to dictate who we are by their words. As humans, we tend to wallow in self-pity. We feel sorry for ourselves and can't understand why others don't. But we need to understand that we do have power, we just need to use it for our better good. Now, this doesn't mean that you become the bully, it means you step above it and become a better person because of it.

You may be saying to yourself, "yeah easy to say for you. You're an adult and get to do whatever you want." True, but I was once a teen and believe it or not, I was made fun of horribly in school. I was called names from 4-eyes, bubble butt, Dumbo the elephant, stupid, ugly, worthless…..I've heard them all. And I allowed many of these names to defy who I was, until one day I realized that the only one who can take back my personal power was me. I started working on improving myself. I started reading self-help books, I started looking at magazines to see what style was going to be mine, I started building my self-esteem up with self-talk chats in the mirror. Yes, I said it. I had pep talks with myself in the mirror. But you know what? I got my personal power back. I became the one that others wanted to hang out with and be around. I became the one my friends looked up to. But before I went down this path, I also became a bully. At one point, I figured if I couldn't beat them, I would become them. But all this did was make things worse. I felt even worse than before and instead of getting my personal power back I was highjacking others. I was forcing my power on others and began to see the horrible person I had become. That's when I started reading the self-help books and having the pep talks in the mirror with myself. I realized that the only person who could change who I had become, was me. And that's what I did.

But I was also lucky to have a great support system around me. I had my mom to confide in, some of my teachers, and family members. They all allowed me to talk and be heard, and because of this, I was able to work towards becoming a better person, proud to be who I am. You can do the same, but you have to take the first steps.

1. Confide in someone you trust to help you get past the hurt.
2. Check out self-help books from the library. There's a ton of options there. Or online e-books.
3. Write down a list of all your strengths, and yes you do have strengths. It's a list of all the things you are really good at. If you find this hard, then think of the thing's others have said that you are really good at doing. (Example: You make people laugh. You know just what to say at the right time. You are so good with math etc.)
4. Find a school counselor willing to listen and help guide you.
5. Start writing a list of who you want to be and concentrate on all the steps it would take to be that person.
6. Write down positive talk and practice it in the mirror. (Example: I'm a beautiful person. I love the way my hair looks. I love to help others. I love my body just the way it is. People like to spend time with me, because of my cheery personality etc.)
7. Remember that no one can change you, only you can do that. And no one can define who you are, only you can do that.

How to Get Your Story Across.

Many times, when you start sharing it can become difficult to convey what you are going through or how you feel. But you want to ensure you are heard. I have a few recommendations to help you pull your story together, to convey it completely when you do share with someone you trust.

- Write a list of all the things that have conspired.
    - Words thrown at you
    - Text messaging
    - Posts on your social channels
    - Rumors that you've been made aware of
- Ensure you've saved the text messages sent.
    - You can set up a folder to keep them all in one place
- Save any posts that have come across your social channels.
- Write down rumors said, and who shared them with you.
- Now pull it all together in a way, I like to refer to as a brain map.

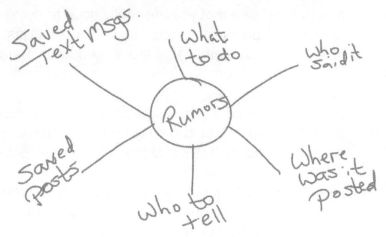

- Once you pull this together decide on who you plan to share this information with.
    - Remember that they need to be someone you trust, who can help you find ways to deal with both the feelings you are having and how to move forward.

By doing these simple things you will be better prepared when sharing your story. This will also help you get better resolution for all involved. This isn't a way to get revenge or do harm towards those you feel hurt you, it is a way to resolve the issue for all. It is a way to get to the bottom of your hurt and get on a path of healing for everyone involved. Because there are no winners in the game of bullying, no matter what you may think.

Going Offline Is Not a Bad Thing

One of my best recommendations is to go off-line. That means turn the phone off and don't check your posts. This can many times help you to take a step back and get away from the hurt. But you have to be willing to let it go. That means willing to not check your phone to see if they texted you again or maybe one of your friends has an update. It will simply put fuel to the fire. Unless you like being hurt and reading all the hurtful things said about you.

You have to remember that you are accountable as well. Your accountability is whether you plan to keep it going or refuse to and shut down your phone and computer. Here's a thought, as soon as you are done with your homework, watching TV, raiding the frig, bugging your sister or brother, go outside. Breath the air, look around you, take in the colors of your surroundings, count the birds, go for a walk; in other words, get away from the electronics. And no, this is not the time to stew on what was said earlier in the day or think about great comebacks. It's a time for you to regenerate your brain, turn off your day, hit the restart switch. Whatever that may be to you.

Empower Yourself

The only way we can empower ourselves is to stop the chatter in our heads. To quit listening to that little voice fueling our fears. Because whether you want to believe it or not. The only way you become empowered is to let go of your fears. As we covered in a previous chapter, fear is the main reason people do much of the things they do. Bullies are bullies due to their own fears of being rejected or hurt. When we fear of being un-liked or losing our friends, we allow fear to take over, losing your power. And I know this is hard to hear, but the only one who can control this is YOU.

- o Figure out what you are scared of
    - o Losing your friends
    - o Being made fun of at school
    - o Beat up
    - o No one will listen
    - o No one will care

All of these are fears based on misconceptions or ideas that you have allowed to fester in your mind. As I've mentioned before, fear is simply based on unknown factors or stories made up in your mind based on words. That's right, words. What do bullies do best? They use their words to hurt others, and when you allow this hurt to penetrate you, and get to your core, you allow your power to be given over freely to the bully. Let's break this down:

Words are not a thing, place or object. They are used to convey a story, tell someone you love them, help someone feel special, make someone feel better, but we can also allow these to define us. When was the last time your mom told you she was upset with you? When was the last time a friend said they were mad? As we use words to express our feelings, we tend to attach feelings to many words. Words can make us feel warm, comforted and strong. They can also make us feel hurt and despair. It just depends on the words we use. But imagine if you used words without any inflection in your voice? Imagine if you said to someone, "I am mad at you" in a mundane voice filled with boredom. Would you take those words to heart? No, because they wouldn't be the same thing without the feelings that are behind those words, which is what we call reflection.

Here's a little exercise to get what I mean. Have a friend or family member help you with this little exercise. Close your eyes and have them say in the most boring way possible that you are a wonderful person. Now have them do the same thing only with meaning behind it. Can you hear and feel the difference these words have based on the inflection in their voice? This rings true with any conversation. If the words that are being said mean nothing to you, then they can't make you feel bad or good dependent on what's said.

As a society, we tend to give words new meaning simply by the way we say them. Next time someone says something hurtful, is it the words that hurt or the way they said them? And if these words hurt, why did they affect you so much? Do you really believe them?

With this in mind, you can do the same thing with words when you are dealing with a bully or someone who says hurtful things to you. Imagine you have a shield on your heart that is impenetrable. Absolutely nothing can get past this shield. Now when someone says something hurtful, imagine that those words are bouncing off your shield, like a superhero. They don't affect you at all. You see, it's all how you look at it. But with this comes practice. Practicing putting up your shield, practicing not being affected by the words, practicing walking away because it doesn't matter to you.

Now, this doesn't mean you become the bully and start throwing words at everyone else because your shield is protected and can't be affected. It simply means that you look at these words differently. That words are just that, words. They don't mean a dang thing unless you allow them to take on meaning.

By believing in these words, you give them power, thus why bullies exist. They gain their power by taking away yours. Which is why it's very important to protect your power, empower yourself, believe in yourself, and believe in the strength each of us has to offer.

Trust me when I say, I get it and know what it feels like to be bullied. But I also rejoice in the feeling of empowerment and the realization that everyone has only one job to do in this life; live it. Live it to the best of your ability and realize that things come up, life throws you punches, lemons, curve balls, whatever the issue, it's a matter of preservation. To realize that everyone deserves to be happy and live their lives the way they chose to.

There's Two Sides to The Bully, Actions, and The Human Side

When it comes to bullies realize that there is a human inside hurting just as much as you, maybe even more than you know. Because bullies aren't made overnight, it takes months or sometimes years of hurt and pain.

When we all come into the world it is not our destiny to become a bully. Bullies are a product of their environment. An abusive parent, either physically or mentally, years of hurt from school mates, a world filled with hurtful words or fists. Whatever the circumstance a bully is simply a person who is so insecure in themselves, they gain power by taking it from others. Does this mean it's right? Absolutely not, but it helps to understand the person behind the behavior. Because a bully is based on fear, and fear is based on insecurities, and insecurities are based on words or actions. You see where I'm going with this?

Am I saying that bullies don't deserve to face the music or pay the price for their actions? No, I simply want to point out that at one time or another we have bullied someone.

The definition of a bully is "use of superior strength or influence to intimidate (someone), typically to force him or her to do what one wants." If you read this definition and think back to when you were a small child or maybe even to recent events, can you really say that there was never a time when you tried to intimidate your mom into saying yes to you going to the party by using guilt? Or maybe you made your sister hand over her plate of food when you proceeded to explain how spaghetti looked like a plate of worms and blood? Or maybe the time you told your friend that if they didn't go to the movie you wanted to see you planned on spilling the beans on who really broke the taillight on Mom's new car. All of these are ways of getting someone to do what you want them to do, is it not? In a sense, we have all either been bullied or have bullied someone else to get our way, however innocent it may seem. Now does this mean we are bullies? Absolutely not, it simply means that we can't judge others until we take a look in the mirror at ourselves. Does this mean that a bully is not a big deal? Again, NO. I just want to point out that behind that bully is a human being, whether that be a nice person or not, the bully is depending on you to give up your power and submit to what they want you to do. Whether that be to inflict hurt with their words or physical hurt with their fists. However, what bullies do not consider is your strength and tenacity to not give up.

This reminds me of a classic movie, "Cool Hand Luke". If you've never seen it, I highly recommend it. This movie is the perfect example of not giving up or giving in to your circumstances or giving into a bully. In this movie, the main character, played by Paul Newman, is forced to face a big bully. This bully continues to pick on him over and over, but Paul never gives in, to the extent that one day they get into a brawl. Paul is by far outweighed and outboxed by this bully. But he keeps getting up, with every punch the bully puts forth and knocks him down. He keeps getting up. He's literally getting his butt beat to the point where the bully is starting to tell him to just stay down. To not get back up. Just stay down. But Paul just keeps getting back up, over and over again. And continues to get beat over and over. But this bully no longer sees Paul as a threat, but a friend as he realizes his inner strength.

You must realize that bullies take on many forms but know that they are human as well. They hurt too, and yes; they have feelings as well. They may hide them really well, but they are there.

The next time you come across a bully, don't be afraid, be strong. Know that words are words until you give them meaning. Until you take them to heart and let them pierce your heart. Know that you, and only you, have the power to walk or run away. You have the power to be fearless and not fearful. It's simply up to you.

Here are a few websites that may help:

- o www.pacerteensagainstbullying.org This is a great site that gives some insights on how to stop bullying.

- o www.pacer.org/bullying/ is another informational site with some great info.

- o www.kidshelpphone.ca is a resource where they've broken it down by age appropriateness.

- o www.nasponline.org which is the National Association of School Physiologist. This is good for parents as it covers many topics including bullying.

- o http://theawesomeanthem.com this is a great video source when you really need a great champion on your side.

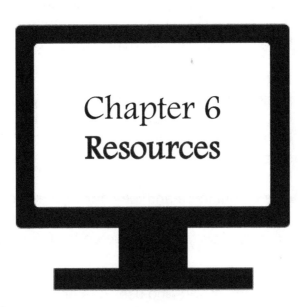

Chapter 6
Resources

Chapter 6 – Resources

I'm a true opponent on gaining the resources you need in order to get the tools you need for any circumstance. With this said, I want you to not only walk away with more knowledge but the tools to help you preserve and keep yourself safe. With this said, here is a list of great resources that I have found over the years that I hope will help you on your journey to online safety.

Here's some quick tips:

- o It's imperative for you to have strong passwords in place. Most good passwords will include a capital letter, lowercase letters, numbers, and characters such as the ($) dollar sign, (@) amper sign, (*) astric, etc. For example: J845$hoN@2850.

- o Find yourself a password software to house all of your passwords so that when you access your accounts the password is filled in for you. This way you don't have to remember them all and they are all kept safely in one place. I personally use Roboforms ~ http://www.roboform.com/, but there are many other options out there and they don't have to cost anything to use. But keep in mind that many of the free options will only allow you to house up to 10 passwords at a time.

- o For those of you who use PC's ensure you go through the updates when they come across. I realize that this is a pain, but what's more important? Protecting your information or taking a few minutes out of your schedule to do the updates? If you have a lot of work to do I recommend you do your updates at night before you shut down. If you have an Apple computer, this shouldn't be an issue.

- o Have a good virus or malware software installed on your computer. I personally recommend AVG ~

Common Sense Test – Do You, Have It?

I used to think that common sense was an inherent trait that we are all born with. However, as I grew up I realized that this is not the case. That common sense is something that is taught by our parents, teachers, counselors, bosses, peers or friends. It is something we must all learn. But before we can learn this we need to first understand it.

The definition of common sense is "good sense and sound judgment in practical matters." In other words, before we do anything we must reason with ourselves as to what the consequences may be with any action we take. In simple words, that I use to instill in my own son, think before you talk, think before you walk, think before you act. Every action we take in life comes with a price or reward dependent upon what that action may be.

Let's see how much common sense you have by taking the following test in the below link:

http://www.allthetests.com/quiz03/dasquiztd.php3?testid=1032140349

Problem Solving Test

Okay now that you've finished with the common-sense test, now it's time for the problem-solving test:

http://psychologytoday.tests.psychtests.com/bin/transfer?req=MTF8MzIwMXwxMjA5MTQzMHwxfDE=&refempt=

Keep in mind that these tests help you to decide, not that you are good at taking tests, but if your mind is in the right place for the right reasons. The reason I bring this up is that many times when we are faced with a decision to make, unless we have all the facts, we tend to feel uncomfortable with that decision. However, many times it takes both common sense and problem-solving skills to help you make a good decision, whatever that may be.

These simple tests don't define you; they are simply meant to help you think about any problem or issue that may arise in your life. By knowing how you fair, it will help you figure out how you manage when it comes to making simple decisions. If you find you don't like the answers, then maybe it's time to ask yourself why. What can you do to help yourself make better decisions? This can help you not only in life but with how you deal with conflict. As you mature, so does your ability to deal with what life may throw your way. Just remember, your decisions are your own and you need to take responsibility for these decisions, good or bad. Once you can own up to your choices you can learn from the lesson, helping you tackle the next in a much better way.

I put this section in because I think it's important to have a starting point so that you can decide what you need to do, if anything, to help you better cope with the day to day stressors. Life will always throw you curve balls, it's what you do with that curveball that really matters. How you handle yourself or how you can improve will help you make better decisions before you post, text, or even open your mouth to speak. This is what we call thinking before you talk. Like I mention in previous chapters, you want to think about what you're going to say or do before you do it. I realize that there may be times when you have to react quickly, but by thinking about the consequences each time before you act, it will help you to hone your quick reflex thinking and allow you to make better choices. Remember, every choice has a reward or consequence dependent upon the circumstance or issue.

TIP: *When making choices remember how it feels when you make a good one vs. a bad one. Based on how this makes you feel will help you to trust your gut. In other words: Did it feel good when you made the right choice for you? Or did it make you feel really bad and yucky when you made a bad choice?*

Social Etiquette

A lot of times when you hear social etiquette you think of manners. You hear your mom telling you:

- No elbows on the table.
- No phones at the table we're eating as a family.
- Don't talk back.
- Don't smack your lips when you're eating.
- Say thank you.
- Ask, please.

You've heard them all. But when I speak of social etiquette here I'm talking about how you conduct yourself online. That means the posts that you send across your social channels. Text messages or emails you send to friends or family. Just like your mother or father would tell you, regarding manners, you need to tend to your manners online as well. This means how you word your posts, text, and emails.

Now we've covered some of this in previous chapters, but we'll get a bit more in depth here based on each platform.

Minding your posts, text, and emails:

- Remember that everyone has their own opinion on things, including you. This does not mean you need to push your opinion on anyone else. When you receive a post that you don't necessarily agree with, this doesn't mean you berate the person posting it. You can still note your disagreement without being mean or brash with words. Remember that not everyone will see eye-to-eye. But noting your comments based on how you feel will help put your point across without pointing fingers.

  For example: Personally, my feeling is that...... This way you are taking ownership of your thoughts without pointing fingers at the sender.

- Don't post with fighting words, as these words can be used against you. Remember how we stated this in previous chapters? The written word can be used in many ways including in a court of law. Choice your words wisely.

- There's no need to post unbecoming pictures with a nasty comment to follow. Even if you don't care for someone, that doesn't mean you have to be condescending or mean.

- Remember what we stated before if you were on the other end of that post how would you feel? If you would be hurt or upset, DON'T POST IT! I get it when there are times you really want them to know exactly how you feel, but remember too, what goes online stays online forever.

- This one is my favorite; if you have nothing nice to say, don't say anything at all. Remember you can be the bigger person here, so be that. Anybody can be mean and say something nasty. It takes a bigger person to do the right thing and just not post, email or text back. By showing constraint you show strength, not weakness. Weakness is allowing them to get to you and getting wrapped into their petty argument or comment.

Here's a new concept that will throw anyone, send them back a compliment. Here's how it might play out:

"You are such a witch. I can't believe they even like you."

"Wow, you really are strong with your words. I bet you would do well in debate class."

"Are you dissing me? Are you calling me names?"

"Absolutely not, just paying you a compliment."

"Why would you do that?"

"Because I believe in using my words wisely, not to be demeaning."

"Are you saying that I'm calling you names and saying that you're stupid."

"Nope. :)"

"You're really weird and not making any sense."

"Sorry, you feel that way. But you have a wonderful evening."

"Are you trying to pick a fight?"

"By wishing you a wonderful evening?"

"Yeah, why would you do that?"

"So you don't want me to be nice to you? You want me to be mean? Now I don't understand."

"Wait, that's not what I said."

"I wished you a wonderful evening and you asked why I would do that,"

"Yeah, but I just called you a witch. Why are you being nice?"

"Because I can."

"What? Are you being snotty now?"

"By saying I can be nice?"

"No, wait you're confusing me."

See how the aggressor now can't understand why you're being nice? My mom always told me that you get more with honey than vinegar, and she was right. By being nice to someone who is coming off being mean, they don't know how to react. They are expecting you to be mad and come at them with harsh words. When you don't, you take their thunder away. How can they respond to someone being nice, especially if they know that they are being mean to you? Do you see how this works? You essentially take the steam out of their anger and confuse them by being nice. I did this to a girl in school one day who had been picking on me for weeks. When she wanted to go to blows. I told her how nice her hair looked that day. All she could say was, "stop being nice to me." And I just keep coming back with, "Why? Don't you think you deserve to be treated nicely?" How can someone really argue with this? They can try, but once others see what's happening, they may chime in as well with, "yeah, she is being nice. Why do you have to be so mean to her?"

By doing this you are negating their words. Their words begin to fall flat. But you also have to say these nice things with conviction. You have to imagine that even though you probably want to pummel them, you are pummeling them with your kind words. It does take practice, so I suggest you do so in the mirror. Pretend you are talking with that person on the other side of that mirror and just throwing mean words at you left and right. But you're throwing niceties at them left and right, while they continue to get confused. After a while, they usually give up because you aren't following the normal weak contender that they are used to pummeling.

Believe me, it works.

 TIP: *Don't let their words get the best of you. Be the stronger contender with your words of kindness and compliments. Trust me, gets them every time.*

Downtime Is Important

This is an important thing to do, and that's to turn it off. Put your phone away for the night with a message that tells your friends you're turning it off for the night and will talk to them tomorrow.

Today many of you have become addicted to your phones, tablets, and laptops. Yes, I said it, addicted. Because that's what it is, an addiction, especially if you can't turn it off. We all need down time. Believe it or not there once was a world where people weren't glued to their phone 24/7. Where they enjoyed their family time with their family. Where they paid attention to the world around them instead of the little screen in their hands.

Why else do you think we have so many health issues today? We don't exercise enough, we don't eat right, we don't pay attention to our surroundings, we don't see what's ahead, we miss what's happening right in front of us because we are so engrossed in our cell phones. Humans weren't made to be on all the time, we need our downtime in order to give our bodies a chance to rejuvenate. When we don't, our bodies and minds suffer the consequences.

I implore you to turn it off, put it down, and look around you. Pay attention to the world that's passing you by, because you are so busy worrying about that missed phone call, you're missing out on everything else around you.

Why Is It Important to Put It Down?

I'll name just a few reasons:

- Mental fog
- Sleep texting
- Insomnia
- Diabetes
- Weight issues
- Getting sick all the time
- Health issues that most doctors haven't seen in years

Besides the above and many more, by putting it down or turning it off you give your brain a chance to reboot as well as your body. Just like your computer, tablet, and phone we all need a reboot giving our minds and body a chance to reset from all the electronic waves. Whether you believe it or not, our bodies and minds weren't meant to be on 24/7. They need rest and relaxation without electronic interference.

Here's a thought….you may not like it….but here it goes: Pick up a book or Kindle, but only for reading not playing games and socializing via social channels. Color in a detailed coloring book. Learn how to paint or play an instrument. Write your first song. Write your first book. Go outside and enjoy nature and all its beauty. These may sound boring, but by doing these simple things you give your mind and body the chance to regroup. You'll sleep better. Learn to appreciate what you have and realize what you're missing when you're glued to your phone, this includes the trees, birds, animals, family, and opportunities to learn new things. But you can't do any of this until you put it down or shut it off.

I get it. This is a really hard thing to do. But take baby steps. Shut it off for at least an hour each day for the first week. Then 2 hours the next week, and so on. Before you know it something magical will happen....you won't miss your phone and will find what the world was like without it....magical.

How

Here are a few steps to help you along the way of shutting down:

- Time your down time on the oven clock or get an egg timer from your local kitchen supply store.
- Start off with 1 hour a day and note it on a paper calendar with a star for each hour of downtime.
- When you go to bed, turn off your phone and plug it in.
- Put it on silent and leave it in your room during family time.
- Find a new hobby, talent or skill that you've always wanted to learn and pay full attention to it without your phone on.

By doing these simple things you will see how much you've really missed. Trust me.

Now we've come to the end of my quest to educate you and give you knowledge about all the different ways to protect yourself from online dangers, device dangers, what to post and not post, and have given you some great resources. The rest of this story now ends with you and the choices you decide to make, keeping in mind, that what goes online stays online forever. See I told I would say it again.

Feel free to share this e-book with friends, your friend's parents, teacher or family members. Pay it forward and spread the word of safety and empowerment.

Thanks for the read and the opportunity to capture your attention. I certainly hope you learned well and took copious notes.

About the author – Katrina R. Garcia

For the past 13 years, Katrina has been helping business owners build and manage both their social media and website presence. However, after holding a safety talk with a Girl Scout Troop, it made her realize how little our kids know about online safety. Thus, the creation of SOS – Social Online Safety. Since this time, it has been her passion to educate everyone on how to protect their data and online image with simple tips that are easy to implement.

How to get in touch with the author:

kgarcia@KGWebsiteDesigns.com

www.KGWebsiteDesigns.com